EXTREME PLACES

The
Deepest
Lake

Other books in the Extreme Places series include:

The Highest Mountain
The Longest Bridge
The Longest River

EXTREME
PLACES

The
Deepest
Lake

Kris Hirschmann

KIDHAVEN
PRESS™

THOMSON

_____✦_____ TM

GALE

San Diego • Detroit • New York • San Francisco • Cleveland
New Haven, Conn. • Waterville, Maine • London • Munich

For more information, contact
KidHaven Press
27500 Drake Rd.
Farmington Hills, MI 48331-3535
Or you can visit our Internet site at http://www.gale.com

LIBRARY OF CONGRESS CATALOGING-IN-PUBLICATION DATA

Hirschmann, Kris, 1967–
  The deepest lake / by Kris Hirschmann.
    p. cm. — (Extreme places)
Summary: Describes the history, geography, animals and plants, measurement, exploration, and ecology of Russia's Lake Baikal.
Includes bibliographical references (p.   ).
    ISBN 0-7377-1372-0 (hardback : alk. paper)
    1. Baikal, Lake (Russia)—Juvenile literature. [1. Baikal, Lake (Russia)]
I. Title. II. Series.
  GB1756 .B33 H57 2003
  551 .48'2'09575—dc21

                                                    2002008579

Printed in the United States of America

Contents

Chapter One
  The Pearl of Siberia   6

Chapter Two
  Studying Baikal   14

Chapter Three
  Life in the Lake   24

Chapter Four
  The Fight Against Pollution   32

Glossary   42

For Further Exploration   43

Index   45

Picture Credits   47

About the Author   48

The Pearl of Siberia

L ake Baikal, which is located in the Russian district of Siberia, is remarkable in many ways. It is the deepest lake in the world. It is also holds more water than any other lake, and it is by far the oldest lake. Because of its many unique qualities, Baikal holds a special place in the hearts of the people who live around it. The lake's nicknames, including "the pearl of Siberia" and "the sacred sea," reflect the way the Russian people feel about this natural treasure.

Lake Basics

The district of Siberia makes up the midsection of the Russian Federation. Lake Baikal is in southeast Siberia, just north of the Mongolian border. The region around the lake is called **Buryatia**.

Buryatia is a hilly area, especially near the banks of Lake Baikal. The entire lake is surrounded by tall mountains with steep sides. Baikal sits between the mountains in a hollowed-out area called a **rift**. A rift is basically a deep crack in the earth. The rift plunges far below the surface of Baikal, reaching a depth of several miles in some places. The bottom three or four miles are filled with solid matter. The top mile or so is filled with water. The water's

The western coast of Lake Baikal can be seen from the shores of the Ushkany Islands in Russia.

maximum depth is 5,371 feet, which makes Baikal the deepest lake in the world. (The second deepest is Africa's Lake Tanganyika, which reaches a depth of 4,710 feet. The Caspian Sea in southwestern Europe/southeastern Asia is third at 3,360 feet.)

Lake Baikal is shaped like an uneven crescent. The crescent is 395 miles long and averages 30 miles in width, and it runs roughly from north to south. This huge sliver of water has a surface area of more than 12,000 square miles. It contains thirty islands, including one that is home to more than five hundred people.

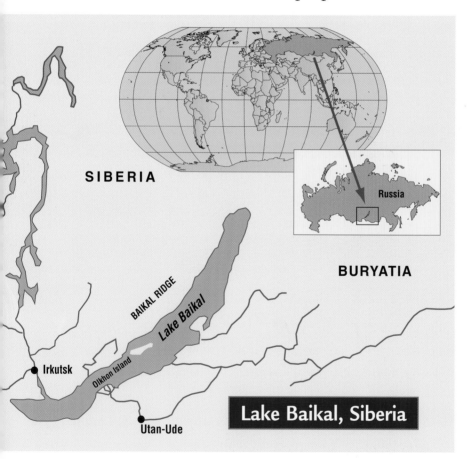

SIBERIA

Russia

BURYATIA

BAIKAL RIDGE

Lake Baikal

Olkhon Island

Irkutsk

Utan-Ude

Lake Baikal, Siberia

A view of Lake Baikal in winter shows the point where it meets the Angara River, the lake's only outward-flowing river.

Freshwater Champion

Lake Baikal is not the world's biggest lake in terms of surface area. Seven other lakes look larger when drawn on a map. In terms of water volume, however, no other lake on Earth comes close to Baikal. Lake Baikal holds about 5,500 cubic miles of water. That is more than 20 percent of the freshwater on the earth's surface.

To help people understand how much water Lake Baikal truly holds, scientists have come up with some interesting statistics. For instance, all five of North America's Great Lakes could fit into the area occupied by Lake Baikal with room left over. Also, it would take almost a year to fill the lake if every river and stream in the world ran into the empty Baikal basin.

Lake Baikal's enormous volume is partly due to the system that feeds water into the lake. Three hundred thirty-six rivers pour into Baikal, but only one—the Angara River—flows outward. With so much water coming in and so little going out, the lake fills more quickly than it empties. However, a lot of the lake's water escapes, or evaporates, into the air. **Evaporation** partly balances the inflowing water and helps the lake's water level to stay steady.

The Birth of Baikal

Another important balance is provided by Baikal's geology. Lake Baikal sits in an area where the land is moving in a way that causes the lake to grow. Baikal's continual growth creates more room for the water flowing inward from the lake's feeder rivers.

How is growth happening? The rift that forms the Baikal basin is actually a place where two parts of the earth's crust are pulling away from each other. The land to the left of the lake is pulling westward, and the land to the right is pulling eastward. This movement is very slow but steady. Little by little, it is yanking the shores of Lake Baikal apart. Scientists estimate that Lake Baikal widens by about one inch per year. It also grows deeper over time as the rift cuts farther and farther into the earth's crust.

Lake Baikal was born many millions of years ago when the rift first began to form. At first the lake was small and shallow, and the land surrounding it was flat. But over time, the earth's movement slowly wrinkled the land around Baikal into mountains and gouged a deep crack beneath the lake. The result is Lake Baikal as it appears today.

The Oldest Lake

Today's Baikal is remarkable not just for its depth and volume, but also for its age. Researchers estimate that

White rocks shimmer along the shore of Lake Baikal as a steep mountain stands tall behind them.

Campers gaze across the expanse of water that constitutes the world's deepest lake.

Lake Baikal is between 25 and 30 million years old, which makes it by far the oldest lake on the planet.

Baikal's age is unusual. The life span of most lakes is only ten thousand to twenty thousand years. A lake "dies" because the rivers that feed it carry dirt, **silt**, and other debris that eventually get dumped into the lake basin. After a while the basin fills with solid matter, and the lake dries up.

The rivers that feed Baikal carry plenty of silt, and

they have dumped a lot of solid matter into the Baikal basin over the years. But the lake's basin has not filled. This is because Lake Baikal is growing fast enough to stay ahead of the silt deposits. As long as Baikal keeps getting deeper and wider, it will absorb the rivers' deposits, and it will continue to grow both larger and older.

A Popular Spot

The wonders of Lake Baikal are well known across Russia. From the time they are small, Russian schoolchildren are taught about the lake and its many special qualities. As a result, many Russians want to visit Baikal and see it for themselves. This desire has created a booming tourism industry around Baikal. During the summer, tourists flock to Buryatia to sit on Baikal's shores, swim in its waters, and travel across its surface in tour boats.

Because Lake Baikal is unusual in so many ways, it is also a magnet for scientists from around the world. Much is already known about Baikal, but there is a great deal still to learn about the world's deepest lake. With time and study, researchers hope that Lake Baikal will reveal more amazing secrets to the scientific community and the world.

Studying Baikal

Russian scientists have been studying Lake Baikal for hundreds of years. Until recently, however, foreign scientists were not welcome in the Baikal region. Also, the world scientific community had a hard time getting Russian scientific records. For these reasons, not much was known about Lake Baikal outside of Russia.

This situation changed in the early 1990s, when Russia finally opened its doors to outside scientists. Today scientists from all over the world travel to Siberia to study Lake Baikal. As a result, knowledge about the lake is increasing and spreading.

This knowledge, however, has not been easy to gain. Explorers stumbled on Baikal in the 1640s while searching

Taken from the space shuttle *Endeavor*, this image shows an aerial view of Lake Baikal during winter.

for gold, silver, and other natural resources. Rough maps of the area were drawn, and many plant and animal species were discovered and named. But efforts to study the lake's size, depth, and climate progressed slowly.

Difficult Conditions

Conditions on the lake were a big part of the problem. The depth of Baikal's waters made the lake hard to study in the early days, and so did the large size of the lake. The first Baikal scientists did not have modern equipment and boats to help them with their work. So getting around on Baikal was slow and difficult, and studying its depths was nearly impossible. Some work could be done by dragging nets and lines through the water, but these methods were neither predictable nor reliable.

Baikal's location, too, was a problem. When it was first discovered, Lake Baikal was thousands of miles from any town. The distance made the lake very difficult to reach before the days of modern transportation.

The harsh Siberian winters were (and still are) another obstacle. Average December temperatures on some parts of Lake Baikal are frigid—15° below Fahrenheit—and the cold lasts for months on end. Because of the cold weather, the surface of Lake Baikal freezes solid around December or January and stays frozen until April or May. Ships cannot travel on the lake during the iced-over period, so research time on Baikal each year is limited.

Unpredictable storms are yet another problem on Lake Baikal. Strong winds sometimes blow up in a matter of minutes. They can reach speeds higher than one

Fishermen race to reach land to avoid being hemmed in by ice on Lake Baikal.

hundred miles per hour, which is faster than a medium-strength hurricane. These vicious winds whip the water into enormous waves that can easily sink ships. Many people, including some researchers, have lost their lives during the lake's storms.

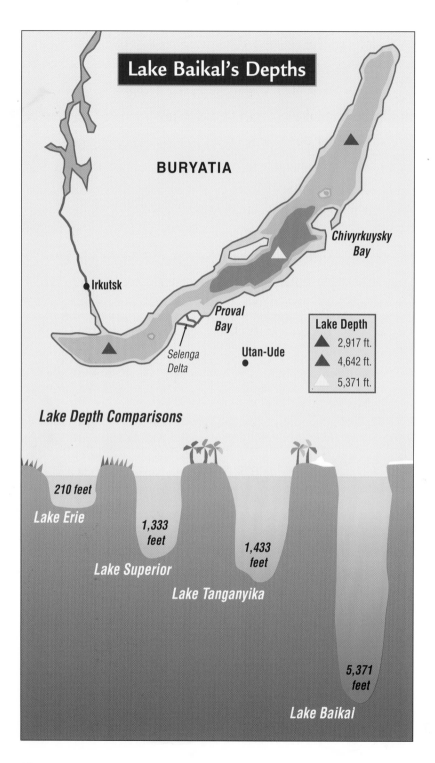

Luckily, the many difficulties of working on and around Lake Baikal have not stopped scientists. Since the earliest days of Baikal exploration, researchers have understood the lake's importance. They have made great efforts to continue their studies.

Finding the Depth

The earliest attempts to find Lake Baikal's depth took place in the mid-1600s. Scientists tied a lead weight to a rope, then lowered the weight into the water. When the weight hit bottom, the scientists planned to mark the rope and measure how much line they had let out. This technique did not work as planned. Reports from 1675 show that many measurements as deep as six hundred feet had been taken in the middle of the lake, but no weights had reached the bottom.

Using the weight-and-rope method, scientists finally hit bottom in 1798. The maximum depth found at that time was 4,062 feet. This number was not the final word, though. Other scientists hoped they might find deeper spots. Therefore many more lead-weight measurements were made in different parts of Lake Baikal. Many depths were found. But because the results varied so wildly, no one number could be considered the "official" depth of the lake.

Modern measurements were finally made by a Russian research ship between 1957 and 1962. Instead of dropping weights, the ship bounced sound waves off Baikal's floor. The reflected sound waves were then "read" to create a map of the lake bed. This is known as **seismic profile**. The profile shows that Baikal has three distinct basins. The deepest one is in the middle of the lake. It reaches a maximum depth of 5,371 feet. Because the profile showed every inch of Lake Baikal's floor, scientists could finally be sure that they had found the lake's deepest spot.

The Limnological Institute

Possibly the most important advance in Baikal exploration was the creation of the Limnological Institute in Irkutsk. Founded in 1928, the Limnological Institute is a branch of the Russian Academy of Sciences. It was built to provide a permanent scientific station on Lake Baikal for a handful of scientists. Thanks to the institute, ongoing studies on Lake Baikal were finally possible. With this advance the pace of research and discovery picked up.

The Limnological Institute became even more important in the early 1990s, when foreign scientists began to enter Russia. The institute became the contact point for scientists all over the world, and it grew quickly. Today the Limnological Institute employs more than three hundred scientists, technicians, and engineers. It also houses a fleet of seven vessels. These vessels are equipped for sampling living plants and animals, water, and bottom sediments in Lake Baikal.

Studies Today

Working through the Limnological Institute, foreign scientists have contributed a great deal to the study of Lake Baikal. They have brought fresh ideas and modern equipment and techniques to the Baikal area. They have also supplied a much-needed flow of people and money. As a result, scientific activity on the lake has increased steadily.

Research today is focused on a few main areas. Scientists are working to learn more about Lake Baikal's plant and animal life. A major drilling project is also going on to help scientists learn more about Baikal's geology and

In recent years, foreign scientists have brought much-needed money and equipment to the Buryatia region.

climate history. Scientists on this project are taking samples of the earth from the bottom of Lake Baikal and examining them in the hopes of finding clues to the past.

Lake Baikal's depth is another area of ongoing research. Although a full map of Baikal's floor has been made, scientists argue that the depths shown on the map might not be correct. They think that the immense water pressure in the deepest parts of the lake could have affected the sound waves used to map the lake's bottom. So studies are being done to learn how sound behaves under

The Russian submersible PISCES waits on the deck of a boat moving across Lake Baikal. The device is used for manned underwater exploration.

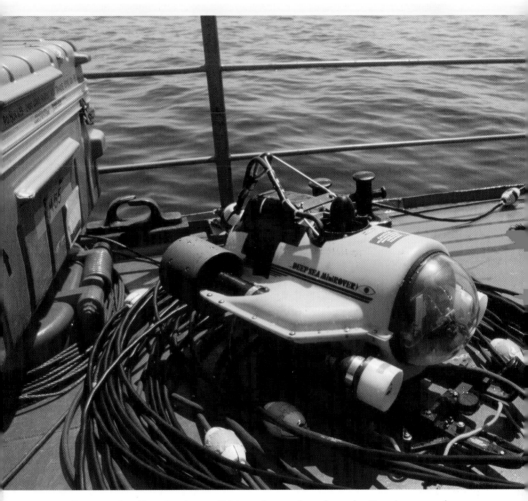

A remotely piloted submersible awaits testing aboard a Russian patrol boat bound for Lake Baikal.

pressure. When these studies are finished, scientists will be able to make better measurements of Lake Baikal's depth.

All of the studies being done today are helping the world scientific community to learn more about Lake Baikal. A great deal has been discovered since the early 1990s, and much more is sure to be learned in coming decades as more scientists study the world's deepest lake.

Life in the Lake

The waters of Lake Baikal teem with life. Scientists believe that the lake contains about eighteen hundred different animal species and hundreds of plant species. Animal species include fish, crabs, worms, sponges, marine mammals, and much more. Plant species vary widely and include several types of tiny plantlike organisms called algae. Algae help to keep Baikal clean and healthy.

The rivers that flow into and out of Baikal do not connect the lake to any oceans or other lakes. This makes it difficult for new species to find their way into Lake Baikal. As a result, plants and animals in Baikal have been able to evolve over millions of years with very little outside influence. About 80 percent of the plants

Green plantlike organisms called algae float near the bottom of Lake Baikal, keeping it healthy.

and animals living in Lake Baikal today are found no-where else in the world.

Special Species

Species that are found only in a certain area are said to be **endemic** to that area. Baikal's endemic species include many unique animals such as the **golomyanka**, the **omul**, and the **nerpa**.

Golomyanka are the most common fish in Lake Baikal. These unusual fish are about ten inches long, and their bodies are see-through. Oil makes up about half of a golomyanka's body weight, so these animals are some-times called "oil fish." Their bodies cannot stand much heat. Golomyanka will die from overheating in water warmer than 50° Fahrenheit, and their fatty bodies will melt like butter if held in a person's hand.

The omul is a type of salmon, and it is the most im-portant food fish in Lake Baikal. It makes up more than 60 percent of the commercial catch on the lake each year. Many lakeside residents also fish privately for this tasty animal. Like salmon all over the world, omul travel up-river to the place where they were born to spawn. Omul eggs take about eight months to hatch into baby fish. The little fish swim back down the river and into the lake to grow into adults.

The nerpa is the world's only freshwater seal, and it is Lake Baikal's only marine mammal. Nerpas are fat, furry animals that grow to just over five feet in length and 280 pounds in weight. They eat mostly golomyanka. No one knows exactly how many nerpas there are, but estimates

Fishermen net a school of omul, which are the most commercially important fish of the Baikal area.

range from sixty thousand to one hundred thousand individuals. Hunters kill about six thousand of these animals each year and harvest their meat, fat, and fur for sale on the commercial market.

Other Notable Creatures

Nerpas and omul are not the only endemic species caught for profit. Grayling, lake whitefish, and sturgeon are also important sources of food. The Baikal sturgeon in particular can provide a lot of meat. In the past, stur-

Sponges dot an outcropping of rock in Lake Baikal.

geons weighing more than 250 pounds were sometimes caught. It seems that the biggest sturgeons have now been pulled from the lake, however, because fish of this size are rarely seen today.

Freshwater sponges are another interesting Baikal life-form. Baikal sponges are green, and they are found from the shallows all the way down to depths of three thousand feet or more. These animals are very common. In some places they sit so close together that they hide the lake floor.

Baikal's sponges provide shelter for hundreds of species of shrimp, crabs, and other **crustaceans** that are found in the lake. Crustaceans are mostly scavengers, which means they look for and eat the flesh of animals that are already dead. By doing this, crustaceans perform an important service: They help to clean the lake bottom.

Lake Baikal also contains many endemic worms that participate in the cleanup job. Seventy species of worms called **oligochaetes** live throughout the lake and gobble garbage off the lake floor. Another type of worm, the flat-worm, takes its cleaning duties one step further. The flat-worm actually hunts for sick or injured animals. When it finds a victim, the flatworm paralyzes it and wraps it in mucus. The helpless prey is then sucked into the flat-worm's mouth and eaten.

Life at All Depths

Life can be found at all levels of Lake Baikal. Nerpa, algae, some types of fish, and mollusks live in the lake's shallow waters. (Mollusks are soft-bodied animals with hard shells. These include clams and snails.) Tiny animals called plankton, some fish, and some crustaceans roam the middle levels of the lake. Certain snails and crabs live only in the deepest parts of the lake. And a few animals, including some sponges, worms, and the golomyanka, can live at any level. They range from the depths of Baikal all the way up to the surface.

It is very unusual for life to exist throughout a deep lake as it does in Baikal. The water circulation in most large lakes is not good enough to carry oxygen-rich water to the bottom zones. As a result, the lower depths are dead regions where no life can exist. In Lake Baikal, however, the annual freezing/thawing cycle helps to keep the water moving. Cold water sinks. So as Baikal's ice cover thaws each spring, the near-freezing (and oxygen-rich) surface water falls downward. This movement forces the warmer water near the bottom of the lake upward. When it reaches the surface, the old bottom water receives a new load of oxygen.

Deepwater Vents

Water-spewing **vents** in some parts of Lake Baikal may also help with water circulation. Scientists discovered these vents in 1990. Sitting at a depth of 1,350 feet, the vents shoot heated water from beneath the lake floor into Baikal's waters. Both the heat and the movement help to keep the water fresh.

Life swarms around Lake Baikal's deepwater vents. Mats of bacteria, small shrimp, and oddly shaped sponges cluster in these regions. Worms, snails, and fish also make their homes near Baikal's vents. Most of the

Hydrothermal vents that spew heated water from the earth have been found in Lake Baikal.

creatures in these regions are bone-white or transparent, and they have poor eyesight. No sunlight reaches these depths, so color and vision are not important to the animals that live here.

Baikal is the only lake where deepwater vents are known to exist. They are common in oceans, though, and are found in areas where new ocean floor is forming. This fact has caused some scientists to believe that Lake Baikal may be more than just a lake. If the Baikal rift continues to widen, they say, then Lake Baikal may someday become the Baikal Ocean. It takes hundreds of millions of years for an ocean to form, however, so major changes will not happen any time soon. For now, Baikal will continue to be exactly what it is: a remote lake that provides a breeding ground for hundreds of fascinating species.

The Fight Against Pollution

L ake Baikal may be the cleanest lake in the world. While the lake holds 20 percent of the earth surface's freshwater, scientists estimate that it may hold as much as 70 percent of the world's *clean* freshwater. The purity of Baikal's waters is just one more thing that makes this lake extraordinary.

Unfortunately, Lake Baikal's remarkable purity may be in danger. In the past few decades, industries along the lake's shores and feeder rivers have dumped waste products into the environment. Many of these waste products end up in Baikal, and they are taking a toll on the health of the lake.

People who understand Lake Baikal's importance are aware of this problem, and they are worried about the lake's future. So they are taking action. Scientists and environmental organizations today are working hard to stop the pollution before it does permanent damage to Lake Baikal.

Crystal-Clear Water

Why is Lake Baikal so clean in the first place? Part of the answer has to do with Baikal's location. The lake is so remote that until recently, human industry and its waste products did not touch the Baikal region.

A chemical plant on Lake Baikal throws smoke into the air.

Much more important to the lake's purity, however, is a creature called the **epischura**. Epischura are crustaceans that look like crayfish, and they swim throughout the waters of Baikal. Epischura are tiny. Their bodies measure less than one-twentieth of an inch from tip to tip. But these animals are everywhere—and they are hungry. Epischura spend most of their time eating. They gobble

Schoolchildren skate across the ice on Lake Baikal at sunset.

down huge quantities of bacteria and algae, thus "filtering" Lake Baikal's water. This natural filter works so well that in some places, Baikal's water is actually cleaner than many types of bottled water.

Not only do epischura purify Lake Baikal, they also make it very clear. It is usually possible to see about 150 feet through the water of the lake. And in the wintertime, Baikal's crystal-clear water freezes into crystal-clear ice. In the cleanest areas, people walking on the frozen surface of Lake Baikal can see fish and other animals swimming many feet below.

The Baikalsk Pulp and Paper Plant

Until the mid-1900s, Lake Baikal remained mostly pure. But this began to change in 1967 when a large pulp and paper plant was built in the city of Baikalsk at the southern tip of the lake. The factory was designed to produce a plant fiber called **cellulose**. Cellulose is used to make paper, clothing fibers, plastics, and adhesives. Unfortunately, making cellulose is a messy business. It involves washing plant matter in chemicals that must be discarded. In the early days of the Baikalsk plant, most of these waste chemicals were simply flushed into Lake Baikal.

Waste chemicals were not the only problem. From its huge smokestacks, the Baikalsk plant also pumped pollution into the air. A lot of this pollution stayed in the air or blew away. A lot of it also fell into Lake Baikal.

Between the flushed chemicals and the airborne pollution, the Baikalsk plant has had a major effect on the southern end of Lake Baikal. More than twenty-five square

The Baikalsk pulp and paper plant, built on the southern tip of Lake Baikal, is responsible for much of the damage done to the lake's environment.

miles of the lake are badly damaged by pollution. At least another eighty square miles are infested by harmful bacteria. As a result, some fish and plant species are dying or dead. Others survive but have trouble breeding in the polluted waters. And day by day, the pollution continues.

Public Outcry

Many people have spoken out about the damage being done to Baikal. These include scientists, writers, fishermen, environmental groups, and other concerned citizens.

The people who live around Lake Baikal care about their beautiful lake. They spoke out loudly against the plant when its construction was first announced. So did a handful of researchers who understood the scientific value of Baikal. When the Baikalsk plant was built, however, there was no active environmental movement in Russia (then called the Soviet Union). Without organized backup, people had little chance of being heard.

But that soon changed. The outrage over Baikal's pollution helped to create a national environmental movement. By working together, concerned citizens drew attention to the Baikal problem. Even some foreign governments and

Mikhail Khlystov lies with his infant twins. The family lives near the lake, which has become polluted by industrial wastes.

organizations joined the battle. Little by little, the objections of the people were heard. By the mid-1980s, the environmental movement was strong enough to convince those in charge that change was needed.

Solving the Problem?

In 1987 the Soviet government finally issued guidelines designed to protect Lake Baikal. The guidelines ended shore logging around Baikal and created nature reserves and parkland around the lake. They also declared that the Baikalsk plant would be converted to harmless activities by 1993. It looked like the Baikalsk problem was coming to an end.

But this turned out to be a false hope. In 1991 the Soviet Union went through huge changes. The entire country, including the Baikal region, became known as the Russian Federation. The Russian Federation had many problems and no money for Baikal. As a result, many important projects were left unfinished.

One unfinished project is the conversion of the Baikalsk plant. So far, the Russian Federation has not found the money to change the plant into something less harmful to the environment. The government also does not want to close the plant, since it makes a lot of money and employs thousands of people. Federal agencies *did* build an expensive cleaning system for the plant, and the system does help to reduce harmful waste. But the Baikalsk plant's basic purpose has not changed. Today, the plant continues to produce cellulose and its waste products continue to pollute the air and water of the Baikal region.

Loads of timber are unloaded at the Baikalsk paper mill.

What the Future Holds

Although the Baikalsk pulp and paper plant is Lake Baikal's biggest problem, it is not the only one. Several large cities along the Selenga River, Lake Baikal's biggest water source, dump industrial and human waste into the river. This waste eventually flows into Baikal. There is also a lot of industry along the banks of the Angara River. Although the Angara flows away from Lake Baikal, airborne

39

Many seek to preserve the beauty of Lake Baikal against the tide of the region's growing population.

pollution from its industries blows back upriver. Much of this pollution falls into the lake.

Baikal's pollution problem is real, and it is growing. Most scientists agree, however, that it is not too bad yet. So far, Lake Baikal's enormous size and its natural filters are keeping the lake clean in most areas. However, Baikal cannot keep healing itself forever. If the pollution does not stop, Lake Baikal may be damaged beyond repair.

But there is hope for Baikal. People around the world are taking steps to protect the lake from further damage. In 1988, an organization called the Baikal International Center of Ecological Research (BICER) was created to study and monitor the health of Lake Baikal. And in 1996 the Baikal area was named a World Heritage Site by the United Nations Educational, Scientific and Cultural Organization (UNESCO). Being a UNESCO World Heritage Site means that Lake Baikal is considered the property of the world, not just of Russia. Therefore all countries are responsible for helping to keep the lake healthy.

So although the pollution problem has not been solved, awareness of Lake Baikal's problems is growing. Perhaps this awareness will lead to greater efforts to protect Baikal. With a little work, the world's deepest and oldest lake should also remain its cleanest far into the future.

Glossary

Buryatia: The region surrounding Lake Baikal.

cellulose: A natural fiber found in plants.

crustacean: A family of animals with external skeletons, including shrimp and crabs.

endemic: Found only in a certain area.

epischura: A tiny crustacean that lives in Lake Baikal and eats bacteria and algae.

evaporation: The process by which water escapes into the air as vapor.

golomyanka: A fatty fish found throughout Lake Baikal.

nerpa: The world's only freshwater seal and Lake Baikal's only marine mammal.

oligochaete: The name given to seventy species of worms living in Lake Baikal.

omul: A type of salmon found in Lake Baikal. Omul are an important food source in Russia.

rift: An area where the earth is spreading apart.

seismic profile: A map made by bouncing sound waves off a surface, then interpreting them with the help of computers.

silt: Very fine dirt.

vent: An underwater crack that spews hot water upward.

For Further Exploration

Books

Nancy Field, *Discovering Crater Lake*. Middleton, WI: Dog-Eared Publications, 1998. Read about Oregon's Crater Lake, one of the world's deepest freshwater bodies. Includes stickers.

Elizabeth Tayntor Gowell, *Fountains of Life: The Story of Deep Sea Vents*. New York: Franklin Watts, 1998. This book discusses deep-sea vents similar to the ones in Lake Baikal.

Sharon Katz, *The Great Lakes*. New York: Benchmark Books, 1998. This book talks about life in and around one of the world's greatest lake systems.

Neil Morris, *World's Top Ten Lakes*. Austin, TX: Raintree Steck-Vaughn, 1997. An illustrated countdown of the world's ten biggest lakes.

Periodical

Don Belt, "Russia's Lake Baikal: The World's Great Lake," *National Geographic*, June 1992. This article is a great overview of Lake Baikal's geology, history, and people.

Websites

Lake Baikal Homepage (baikal.irkutsk.org). The homepage links to information about Baikal's ecology, animals, climate, geology, and more.

Large Lakes of the World (www.infoplease.com). This page lists the world's biggest lakes. Size is ranked by surface area, but figures for length and maximum depth are also included.

Index

algae, 24, 35
Angara River, 10, 39–40
animals, 24, 26
area, 8

bacteria, 30, 35, 36
Baikal International Center of
  Ecological Research (BICER),
  41
Baikalsk, 35
basins, 19–20
Buryatia, 6, 13

cellulose, 35, 38
chemicals, 35
circulation of water, 30
commercial fishing, 28
crustaceans, 29, 30, 34–35

deepwater vents, 30–31
depth, of Lake Baikal
  discovery of, 19–20
  life at different, 29–30
  maximum, 7–8
  research and, 16, 22–23

environmental movement,
  37–38, 41
epischura, 34–35
evaporation, 10

evolution, 24

fish. *See individual kinds of fish*
flatworms, 29

golomyankas (fish), 26, 30
grayling (fish), 28–29
Great Lakes (North America), 10

hunting, 28

industry
  opposition to, 36–38
  pollution from, 35–36, 38, 39
Irkutsk, 20

Lake Baikal
  age of, 11–13
  development of, 10–11
  discovery of, 14, 16
  location of, 6, 33
  purity of, 32
  unique qualities of, 6
  see also depth
lake whitefish (fish), 28–29
life spans, 12
Limnological Institute, 20

marine mammals, 26
mollusks, 29, 30

nerpas (fish), 26, 28
nicknames, 6

oceans, 31
oil fish. *See* golomyanka
oligochaetes, 29
omuls (fish), 26, 28

pearl of Siberia, the, 6
plankton, 29–30
plants, 24, 26
pollution
  airborne, 35
  environmental movement and,
    37–38, 41
  epischura and, 34–35
  extent of, 35–36
  government response to, 38
  lakeside sources of, 32, 35–36,
    38, 39
  location and, 33
  river sources of, 39–40
pulp and paper plant
  opposition to, 36–38
  pollution from, 35–36, 38, 39

research
  Baikal International Center of
    Ecological Research and, 41
  current projects, 21–23
  depth and, 16, 19–20
  difficulties encountered, 14,
    16–17
  foreign scientists and, 14, 20
  Limnological Institute and, 20
  winters and, 16

rifts, 7
rivers
  flow of, 10, 24
  silt deposits from, 12–13
  as source of pollution, 39–40
Russian Academy of Sciences, 20
Russian Federation, 6, 38

sacred sea, the, 6
salmon, 26
seals, 26
Selenga River, 39
shape, 8
Siberia, 6, 16
silt, 12–13
Soviet Union, 38
sponges, 29, 30
storms, 16–17
sturgeon (fish), 28–29
surroundings, 6–7

tourism, 13

United Nations Educational,
  Scientific and Cultural
  Organization (UNESCO), 41

vents, 30–31
volume, 9–10

winters
  circulation of water and, 30
  clarity of ice during, 35
  research and, 16
World Heritage Site, 41
worms, 29, 30

Picture Credits

About the Author

Kris Hirschmann has written more than sixty books for children, mostly on science and nature topics. She is the president of The Wordshop, a business that provides a wide variety of writing and editorial services. She holds a bachelor's degree in psychology from Dartmouth College in Hanover, New Hampshire. Hirschmann lives just outside of Orlando, Florida, with her husband, Michael.